A Cargo Of Balloons
Christopher Philip Sykes

ISBN 1   870016   00 9

OTHER BRANCH READINGS

Printed by Tomes of Leamington

The publisher acknowledges
financial assistance from
West Midlands Arts towards
the publication of this book.

OTHER BRANCH READINGS
2, 46 Willes Rd, Leamington Spa.

CONTENTS

A CARGO OF BALLOONS

So aspiration floats, ascends
in hot balloons green as pears
carrying ex-Himalayan adventurers
(bodies shot and nerve gone)
with their advertisers' and their
sponsors' slogans high into the air
to bulge transparent over car parks,
pine trees and the tented village
and fenced-in cattle of the Royal Show.
From Pirelli, Dunlop, IBM and ICI:
hundreds of silk-frocked secretaries
and girl-fridays released
into the atmosphere: painted ladies
strawberry red and lilac blue,
logos stretched across their chests,
purple shadow on their eyes,
blonde hair lacquered after them
like wisps of air, leaflets
spilling from their hands
like frilled white pants or snow.

Gliding slate roofs and trees,
wind inside their skirts,
they draw golfers' eyes
from off the greens
and ruin critical putts.
In one long second pile up
sixty cars on the Warwick by-pass.
On a smaller scale
cause a police motorbike to collide

with a truck and tip a man
off his bike breaking his skull on a rock
at the narrow bridge at Stoneleigh.

Extended on the blue shadow of evening -
Devastation trailing the Warwickshire meadows
in their wake - men trapped
under tractors, heads and feet
stuck from swallowing combines,
arms and legs sawn off,
boats turned over on the Avon,
ambulance and police flickering
over the hills and sky - they return
newly frocked from the shops
of Stratford and Leamington,
purpled by the beams of falling sun.

Dawdling over populated cricket fields
the rustle of silk and laugh
glimpse up the legs,
still gets the odd batsman out.
Clouds behind them in a backdrop
they hang like varnished Tiller girls
in a long line facing the queues of cars
out of Stoneleigh to the M6 and home.

Then, with the countryside at tea,
dinner, supper or at evening meals,
cars in snug wistaria-festooned garages,
cats on honeysuckled window sills,
night-scented stock beginning to waft
its scent of dolly mixtures
from the villages of Hockley Heath
Hampton Magna, Claverdon to Shrewley,
a few lawn mowers still chugging

fat ex-chief constables up and down
in dusk, some of which they set amok
getting one or two toes chopped off,
a few others lying on their sides
by hedgehogs under privets, motors chugging -
coronaries set off - they wander together
up the long drives of country houses -
an irresistable force: a flock of silk
crunching gravel.

                    Up lines of oak and limes
exuding scent of lilies, orchids,
strawberries, named - Rochas,
Estee Lauder, Cacherel, Mondi and Chanel
where string quartets send out
the sweetened strains of Schubert,
Mozart, Beethoven, an early
unknown Monterverdi, from sponsored concerts
in Packwood House, Charlecote,
Coughton Court and Hanbury,
Daimlers, Rolls, Mercedes
like corralled stallions in the drives.

They sidle through the long shadowed
shrubbery, amble over tartan lawns -
press their silk frocks on the leaded glass,
linger on the terraces outside -
the shapes of tight silk and cotton,
lurex swimsuits stretching over
blonde thighs and bare behinds,
bare necks and backs, shoulders
pearled and jewelled by rising moon -
saying nothing, while the lolling heads
of be-knighted managing directors
of Courtaulds, IBM and ICI

catch their painted eyes -
and the mellowed, varnished music flies.

Powered by the smell of Brut, Stag,
Obsession, filled with the smell
of Scimitar, unable to bend again
to the interval wheel and deal
among the wine and cheese and topiary
of cocks and hens and Grecian Urns
as the balloons give out hot jets
of air and turn irresistably
against the rising pearly moon
the silvery heads all leave their seats,
abandon their abandoned wives
to watching television outside.

A phalanx of men longingly mesmerised,
across the lawns, out through lily ponds,
up to their waists across rivers,
eyes held on the horizon of clouds
and sky, telegraph poles and silken sylphs.
Over fields, chased by bulls,
butted by goats, dinner jackets
and Gucci shoes dripping foul grey mud,
hair smacked down, clothes torn,
trails of puffing men collapsing
over barbed wire in a coronary straggle -
the labels on their jackets flapping
in the wind: a plaintive cry
of bleeping pagers, listened to
by rooks, heads on sides in rookeries.

Miles and miles, Lemming-like
the strong ones go (young businessmen
of the year) to the far off coast

of Wales, faces caked with spit and foam,
to plunge high cliffs over which
the balloons all float serene
and subside finally into the glittered sea,
washed up - hands in a murmuring bulge
of silk - Courtaulds, Pirelli, IBM and ICI.

Meanwhile back at the country houses
waiters and butlers move between
the scattered trays and tables,
plucking glasses like dawn-blushed mushrooms
from the lawns while the gathered heads
of white roses watch recorded highlights
of men's doubles from Wimbledon
introduced by a powdered face
wearing a beret, a string of onions
round his neck, buttering croissants
and just hearing the news of the catastrophe
and the thousands of cameras descending
like rooks in his ear-piece
on Breakfast Time TV.

SUBURBAN SAMURI

I bumped into a man in the train corridor.
I couldn't avoid him or the clear bowls
where his glass eyes swam, like piranhas,
as I imagine them, broken nerve ends
in red pools. He held me in front of him
at the surface of a cool grin. At once
I heard a windless wind howl and shriek.
From the back of his throat heard
the wolf-ache of the world, saw hair
stood up in a shaggy mane down his back.
At the back of his pupils saw lines
of black fields, bonfires and factories
pushing out car windscreens. Saw two
by two terraces, estates fancy-bricked,
Georgian white-gabled bay-windowed car-
porched - cars pouring in and out
of the roads like sweat. The frosted
front doors yawned their shut mouths.

I saw terraced-skulls built on the skies,
piranha mouths opening and closing
in his shaved eyes as I smiled, stood back
and apologised and moved aside so he
could pass. He moved down the corridor
swaying from side to side as if overbalanced
by armour he wore - a samuri beaded with light.
Peasants cowered as the Lord Protector
Of Peasants went past their compartment doors.
As if feeling my eyes on his back
he stood in the light at the end of the car,
his arms moved up from his sides, hands
coming to rest lightly on the handles
of a black brief-case and two swords.

CIRCA 1986

Telegraphs Guardians and Times
paraded like over-sized tickets
for some club - pedigrees
of Crufts' Champion Dogs,
discreet, folded sharp under arms.

No sun mirroring city windows
and walls, picking out
sharp black and white
on this second class train
lit with a pale light.

No men in crumpled macs
(notebooks and cameras to flash?)
offering girls bouncing their tits,
murderers, rapists footballers
and upper-class twits,
fistfuls of salty fish and chips
crumpled on the upholstered seats,
or out in the corridors, hung round
the buffet and toilet doors.

All is more serious here -
the dimmed light of a library
not the Star-light of a fair.
Mouths now used to international
cuisine - lentils, rice, tofu,
chilli con carne, coq au vin.

Accountants, bankers, solicitors,
computer experts, poets, managers
drawn into this glowing metal
and skin vessel of train,
like milk herds from fields.

Through Oxford, Berkshire,
The Home Counties, men
chewing their papery cud,
who climb on each other's shoulders
each day to stack the city
with tall towers - black
and white freesian shirts,
suits of Hereford brown,
in a wisdom of glasses
yawning up into the clouds,
beyond the bridges of Vauxhall
Lambeth and Blackfriars.

At night the lowing leaves off
and the cities fall into dusk,
tall towers dimmed over the dome
of St Paul's as starlings
fly in over night clouds
like torn soot-flakes of moon.

And the day shift of trains
runs away again over estuaries
of rails and the foot prints
of cattle in mud. Gates
bang shut to leave
the heifers and bullocks
once more in tethered fields -
weary ones resting in warm houses,
by the hum of washing machines,

regained into Aaran sweaters
by the pubs and village cricket teams.

In the desolate streets,
lorries and taxis washing by
washed with a grey wash,
white gulls trail fat tugs
of rubbish carts home
to snatch up deciduous bones -
feasting in slime roosts
on carcass of chicken,
parsleyed lamb in bechamel sauce.

City homes glow and windows
wink figures like lights in pools.
And while the countryside dims
its reservoirs of grass verges
and hedges full of yellow-hammers
and grubs, and while power stations
and chemical factories stand
silhouetted with the sun
setting on their towers and gantries
of ribs, the starlings preen
their blueyblack lacquered feathers
like boas up to the chin,
clatter for moments on stilettos,
shriek together for warmth
in Leicester Square while
armfuls of men roll beneath
searching for quality newspapers
to wrap themselves in, chins,
furred grey as dog turds get
in grass, biting back
songs of speckled beer.

NEWSPAPERS ON TRAINS

1

High wings fluttering
over eyelids and brows,
hairpieces, scarves, ears
and toothless mouths. Bankers,
accountants, computer experts
and me. The world's posteriors
floating by, beneath
a stilled lake of trees.

Sunlight shafting through leaves,
curios of spider webs
sprinkled with rain -
filtered light shadowing
the shadows on a woman's face,
a bird in flight, or a man
on his knees.

Faint skeletons traced
in the skins - race-memories
of burial mounds - arms
and legs, severed skulls
hollowed by mould.
Wild flowers, deer
and rabbit dung. A pond
glimpsed through leaves.

Tractors and armies
and bulldozers. The noise
of the world subsides here
in the faint rustling of breeze.

2

Listen to papers on trains.
Listen to them talk to each other
in sideways whispers and sighs.
"I see they've found
more bodies of ash, fallen limbs,
broken skulls, unearthed
in the slow, centuries-old
gathering of peat."
"Look at these wood violets
plucked here in coloured ink."

3

When the facts of the world
are all known, when it's all
written down and reported on,
will the bright feathers of birds -
macaws, parrots and jays
lift their wings solemnly
out of the sheaths of these leaves,
and raise all these faces upwards,
like orchids towards rain?

15

2

LONDON UNDERGROUND

The tube trains wind through slate
from Kensal Rise to Liverpool Street
and are like dreams through lines
of underpants, vests, nighties, negligees,
windows and cut walls of brick - London dreams
clattering out of all the piled-coat
cotton-quilted and duveted beds,
free beyond the flap of skin around
each coiffeured or stubbled head -
a silver sediment moving over the earth
and down into the light - a black man's head
and shoulders in every cab: pulses
of electric leaving the dark earth-mouths
singing, polished silver trails,
half like slugs or snails, tipping down
an incline behind them in the night.

Headlights on. Inside dark tubes
faces bulge to all the glassy
black-furred walls and screech
at all the noise - the sudden loss
of speed, vertigo, and tug to arms and feet.
Then the rushing on that's like
being pushed into a dark drain hole
or wide, deep-throated scream. Bodies
judder. Panicked eyes search busily
for what there is to see and to see
what there is to not see. The bodies
pressed to platforms, the bodies
rocked together in fast space -
smells of bodies, come too close.

Perfumed bodies come too close.
Stale sweating bodies from foreign parts -
Australians Chinese Algerians Scots.
Bodies falling into black pits.
Bodies screeching under wheels.
Bodies in long silk stockings -
smooth-lipped and eggshell-breasted bodies.
Men in bulging tight white underpants.
Hom asses with bulging testicles and cocks.

Garlic-mouths, raincoats and earringed ears.
Men in dresses, bearded men in frocks.
Mouths eyeing each other up through
the wide-brimmed hats of cocktail glasses.
Cavorting pairs of black tits
and round white bums. Women in uniforms
fingers stroking epaulettes.
Legs swinging over black pits
that claw like elastic tied to legs.
Bodies filing past and hands pulling.

               **   **

While up above the eyes revolve and pulse
in lids of skin: the wallpaper shines,
flock or coffee-stained from Highbury
down to Brixton and is neat or grim.
Outside shut windows, in day,
daylight circles the sky with blue
and windless skies, or the black wings
of rooks, springs sparrow-hawks, crows
and gulls to Regents or Hyde Park
for picnics in the grass by Easter lollers
in deck chairs - still the eyelids spin,
green skirts and white arms, heads in

green hoods goose-pimpled in the sun:
SERENITY. The shops of Oxford Street
spin like still pools, when empty,
in which to dip fat feet. And in all
the houses, behind the lighted windows
of the silent facades of stone, brick
and glass hotels - still memories
of honeymoons or weekends, like tall faces
looking out of Park Lane and Marble Arch
where the prostitutes all stand -
no wind skims the white curtains
and only Filipino maids go past.

Light moves softly padding from room
to room like a wet man after a bath
or like a heavy cat - televisions flicker
and the bath water laps in daylight
or the night. Trays on bedside tables
stir as the cat pokes its head around the door -
congealed food is silent on knives and spoons,
though napkins move and toast crumbs shift
like iron filings attracted by its fur.
For open eyes and sweating legs and arms
nothing or no-one is there, though the door
clicks lightly as if a ghost has just gone out.

Where bodies walk out of their clothes
and shoes, still the trains move on and roar
down in the deep earth and out in the air -
from Highbury and Islington to Finsbury Park,
from Kensal Rise to Liverpool Street.
Pyjamas nighties negligees.
Floorboards move beneath the carpets,
shadows haunt the half-clothed light,

in daylight or the night - houses
cut in half by rails, houses back to back,
glasses shivering by bedside lamps -
as the cat stays, padding about
through the tunnel of the day:
chair-legs, piles of clothes on floors,
the legs of chests of drawers.

The bodies slumbering in the sheets,
smooth-skinned, tattooed and bearded,
watches ticking, the bodies shuddering,
the bodies still - the cat stands agelessly
beside the arms and legs and open mouths,
the painted lips, the earrings and the beards,
the smells of sweat: the betrayers,
the lovers and the lost - pants quietly
in the dark and licks its rough tongue
against their salty eyes and lips and feet.

GIRL ON A TRAIN

She left the compartment a schoolgirl
in plum coloured blazer,
pleated skirt and straw hat.
Now she's back a young woman,
décolleté and bangly,
with earrings and beads to match.
INNOCENCE to EXPERIENCE in one go -
more useful than I've thought
the toilets of trains.

Knees up, slightly askew on her seat
she sits praising her deep eyes
with blue dust and a small mirror
as we glide on towards London
just before six. Studying the roof
of the train she lengthens her lashes
with long, slow strokes of a brush.
Bent forward into the glass palm
of her cupped hand she now smears
a red cream - extract of passion flower
thickly onto her lips.

I realise now I know nothing
of girls' silences at school
or at home. The straightforward
sighing of legs, girls arm in arm
in the streets, chattering mouths
thumbing through magazines,
legs kicking undesired on beds.
The between whispering of heads.

Only this world-face connected
with closed doors and running water:
mirrors of denial and lust.
I feel somewhere I maybe knew more
and now it's got forgotten, lost.
Privacies conceal us from ourselves.
Give us strength and leave us alone.

I put down my book and watch.
This is a lesson I learn -
as painters formed by models:
study to know how to see.
Study the quick world brazenly,
it doesn't care. Caught in no moment
but its own so it seems.

                **   **

The cosmetics in glass packets
and tubes look like so many
Swiss sweets, and her movements
between them alluring - the quiet click
of blusher and lipstick:
the still quality of hands.

Long hours of experience in kitchens,
the tops of buses or in back rooms
in front of flickering tv screens
draw between her fingers
with each colour she adds.

All over the world I imagine
women in cardigans are
putting these down - symbols
of imprisonment and liberty -
and meeting the world-face plainly

while, seeing no prison,
she sits picking them up.

The train shivers us together
and apart as a fast train goes past.
The window is shattered with pearls.

Almost complete she pouts herself
into her hand: the reflection
flown free of a ghost-bird over the sea.
In space her red mouth swims perfectly.

Ahead of her a glittery glass sea -
doors of night clubs opening
polished dance floors, champagne mouths
tipped into her glazed mouth,
sequined frocks into which
she subsides. Foamed grey in her wake
the flecked air of speech days,
mothers, fathers, schools?

The worlds she keeps apart,
that yet cling and divide:
Image and Reality. That the light
should always be easy as this
between worlds - her artistic eyes
moving to her chin, brushing,
re-brushing, correcting. And
her long hair flicked back again.

                    **   **

The realm she presses on me.
The far ache of that quick sea,
and the long flight of perfectability!

To keep two in the eye -

the shadow over the ordinary, clear
bottle top popping sea,
and the silvered body itself turning
in the hard glass of dark sun and sky.

IMAGE   -   REALITY

Together and apart
for moments long as I can
to meet two of my faces here, alighted
into the black mirror-screen -
framed in covers of Vogue, Elle,
Harper's Bazaar, Woman -
blusher on my cheeks, blue
shadowing my lids, lipstick
making voluptuous my mouth,
kohl flickering under my eyes,
gull wing back of my head
and my slim body more desirable
like this - so I could recline
on a couch - speeding over a sea
of desires - skirt up over my hips,
feeling the power of lace,
long shapely legs in black nylons
flowing cool into black pencil tips?
In its scattering of pearls,
the still, black eye
of the world eyeing me.

**   **

What photographs from my
opened iris eye as the light
prints itself on me?

Ticket collector bending beneath
my lids? A stranger watching me
with book on the table?
Newspapers prying with heads in between?
The air sweating with the silent,
loud lonely ache of hands for my knees?

And out of the train,
in my skirts racing the streets,
off the ground in my high heels,
hair tossing irresistibly free?
Suddenly anchored in space -
only a camera on legs,
receiver of light, colour, noise -
honked at by lorries,
howled to by cars, hands and mouths
wanting to haul themselves into bed with me?

Are there only pin-holes for light?
Flown face crumpled into the still gloss
of magazine stands? A prelude
of long naked legs? Blown air
inside glittery white dust?
A pool to be dipped in
for reflection? Faces to take snaps
of their own giddy smiles away?

Recede into the streets
such conflations of dreams -
human power compels, divides
snares and impedes.

My eyes narrowed to the thickness
of light I rested my head
back in my seat, was rocked by the train

half asleep with only the aperture
of clear light washing over my sight.
A piece of film on which
two gulls flickered and flew,
together and apart, settling
their images slowly - rising
and subsiding on dust-wings -
turning over acres of town roofs
and streets, arcing in sun
that transforms their wings
as it touches their tips,
gold, diamond blue, pearl -
nails in long polished tips
a red cream brushed to lips,
silk legs trailing out,
skirt up over my hips.

UNDRESSED

To take your clothes off
and put them over chairs
at night, is to know
that yet another day
is now failed and gone.
All aspirations - journeys
wished or travelled on,
scattered into nothing else
but foam. Those still dreams
in the mind with cherished
birds inside - cages opened,
broken.

　　　　To know it will always
be like this - cooling rooms
with empty clothes on stools,
skirts and dresses,
socks and nylons hanging
over backs and arms of chairs.
And the moment's embrace -
glad flesh on flesh.
Curtained twilight.
And the song of birds outside.

FICTION

Sat in bed I read a tale
of the Russian land
on a misty grey Easter Eve.
Ireonim on the black and lapping
waters of the River Goltva.
His ferry rope swung taut,
studded with water drops
like buds along a gnarly rose,
and he hauled his own life,
in flat tarpaulins between his hands,
against the tug of the river stream.

Goats and sheep, boxes, crates,
floating bodies, shapes
of shoulders, backs and heads.
Monastery bells chiming moonlight
on the smooth, dark lake
risen from the river
to submerge allotments,
trees and fields. A town
deep in sleep - moonlight
washing in among the roofs.

Drawing nearer in the dark,
as if lifting his spirits
from a funeral, the ferryman sang
like a rising thrush
of his friend Brother Nikolay's hymns,
while Chekhov stood braced
into the dark night wind,
five copecks in his hand
with which to pay him.

27

TRIBAL INSTINCTS

Drifting, on the edge of sleep,
sleep of deliverance
that is not death,
in warm pillow, cotton sheets,
as in a bed of heather by the sea
doors start to open and bang
beneath me.

Born of the eternal light
creatures of the light
laugh and shriek, pull chains,
chase each other, slam doors
as if throwing boulders
into a still lake-skin
just to see the blackness
refract, shatter and spin.
Primitive instincts win.
Now the tribal dances thump
through several floors.
Living in a shared house
what can you do, except
wait for them to rest,
so you can too?

And will life live on in noise?
To light up all the darkness
of this world with cars,
electric light and stereos?

I'll have to go down there again,
wrapped in a blanket,

stand at the door and say -
light is like a million herrings,
oily backs flickering beneath
the blue green surface of the sea.
Fish that offer silver
on their sides - mirror fish
of the sea. As they all gather
at the door, curious
in their young, blasé way
to laugh, make comments, gesticulate -
lift the grey sea-scape of my arms
for stars to wink and coalesce:
silence them with shoals
of moonlight, not complaints.

INSOMNIA - OR THE HOUSE ASLEEP

Heads are like houses
it seems to me. Even when
all is quiet, lights off,
all doors bolted and I
settle down to sleep
some sound can begin
to rock in me - like wood
clicks and breathes,
like the house itself
will stretch
and in stretching
find its ease.

Down a passage,
several floors below,
somewhere in the dark,
a noise begins, clear and faint -
(scratching of an insect
trapped rodent or a bird?
Water up from the basement
liquid shadows placing
footsteps on the stairs,
carrying darkness upwards
to my door? Burglars
or criminals forcing entry?
Things to terrify me?)

Listening, a great silence
dwells in every cavity
of my thoughts.

I am convinced by now
it is the noise of some
Eternity crept inside
the creeping of my ear,
that in stillness
out of the noise of the day
is ready, and more ready
than ever, to rest and hear.

For in the hours of half-light
when I am still awake
and am like a log
insensible in the arms
of the Great Ocean Sleep,
I've watched the free world
busily thread itself
with all its ice of light,
and lie fatigued by splendour,
my eyes burned clear white -
bright.

       I watch the birds
that enter and leave glass
by the window sill.
Sprung from forests
that shape themselves
from dark. Forests
that are not forests,
that root in dark and lift
their leafy heads in light
their shadows etched from air
as if on iced-lake skins -
I hold their coldness
for a moment still

3

like a screen around me
then they dissolve
and float again into the light
that is so placid, white and thin.

Dark iced pools and forests
I do not look in.
A thin grey dome of sky
I pass beneath - piled with snow,
engraved with traced white edges
and light, and boats passing
past mine low to the surface
of its skin, oars dripping
iced water, darkened heads
and people in.

Passing through their mouths
and hands ice-shards
smooth and hard
and not begun to melt.
A still, silent world -
sandwiches, oranges, flasks,
steam from coffee, tea
packed for a long journey.

Prints and flowers,
fleur de lys, the earth's
re-birth of ecstasy.
All night and into
early morning light
still birds flying
silent and serene.

LOGGING

We've all done this
haven't we? Sat
transfixed by logs
in grates and stoves
as if in unsought
stillness that throws
its arc of warmth
around us and draws us
quietly into itself
as we go walking by.
Seen faces, arms
and legs of family,
friends, people we
don't know - formed
out of flame, and logs,
when you first look,
firm as those in
fields still covered
in bark or a sheen
of wet, green moss,
black leaves or snow
where you first
picked them up.
Sound of falling earth,
sound of rain, sound
of voices, sound of logs,
sound of near off dogs.
Held in flame
the incidental moments
remain. Until you poke
these memories with a rod

and then they fall
and let out all the heat
that has perservered
with them like faces
wrapped against the cold.
And you see then
the scattered fragments
of the earth and, before
it is extinguished
by the air, the flame
itself that is the glow
of something else,
that burns its own shadow
in space, feeds on itself,
upward, rising, playing
on the surfaces of the air.
The free flame that holds
in place the semblance
of itself, against
the chimney - flame
so certain of itself
becoming blue red yellow
mauve and no matter -
for moments only, then
moments again, always
springing somewhere else -
lower down, beneath
that ash you lift or this.
Throw another log on.
Call in that pair of legs
that's just gone upstairs.
Damn the neighbours.
Let them say tomorrow
we've burned our wood
and scattered white ash
everywhere, over all
the flowers, shrubs, lawns.

A SECOND LOOK

A half a ton of white cast iron
in the centre of one wall -
and a beautiful design:
four white doors with black handles.
Oven top trimmed with black.
Silver towel rail. Wide, black
chimney pipe slotted in the wall.
White hot plate lid by which
the kettle sings - a bird, legs up,
hovering just above the heat.
Above it, clothes hang, like bats
in a cave, upside down,
cobweb-wings that ripple
invisible bands of heat. The stove
stands alone, still, cool and hot
inside. In other words - complete.

It has some negatives.
The salesman never said
when it was bought, brand new
(when there were two wages coming in),
that there would be so much ash
to take away each day.
I've learned about ash now.
It floats up in the air
in a fine dust that you can't
always see except when sunlight
spangles it like a fleece.

It is too an ordinary nuisance.
It encourages colds. It makes me sneeze.

It settles on the frieze
around the walls, half pleasing
with its capacity to pick out
all the ledges in relief. It falls
in a film to books, plates, to everything.

I could tell ash if you gave it to me
in little hand-held clumps.
The ash from smokeless fuels
is heavy, dense, dark or reddish brown.
Throw it on the garden in the winter
though it makes snow sizzle
it's still there, unabsorbed in Spring.
As if Nature has no taste for such
an alien, uncompelling human thing.
And ash from logs is white,
feathery as wedding veils
that float off so easily on wind.

Nor when I think of it
did the man in Kidderminster say
that the white sheen promised "impervious
to heat and easy to wipe clean"
would one day bear so many marks
faint and deeper on its skin.

The monumental accidents that crawl on us.
I can barely tell them in the cracks.
Spilt gravies, broken plates,
cooked chickens, apple sauces, cakes,
blistered fingers, cries and yells.
Easters Christmases, family visits,
faces of mutual friends.
Rivers of bacon grease annealed

beneath the glaze I touch now
and, in habitual response,
remove my fingers from. But then
I put them back because,
to my surprise I see, untended,
the fire's gone out and the stove
is, after all, cold not hot.

'ANTAR AND 'ABLA

The still desert winds.
Thirty of three hundred brigands
all night on their horses
ready at any moment
to turn tail and dash,
watching the bulk of dark -
the creak of armour,
the black horse, Abjer,
shifting on his hooves.

Antar the Moor, spear tip
in the soil, guarding
the narrow mouth to the Valley
of Gazelles while his beloved
Abla, in her litter,
quickly slips away,
across the desert sea
and to the tribes of Abs and safety.

When the dawn rises
through the night and lifts
the coming sun, which, when it's
halfway on its course
across the sky, will make
the sand of the desert
burn like beaten steel,
Antar's armour will remain erect -
a warrior, resting on his spear,
letting his horse breathe.

But the last moments will

have come to Antar
long before the night.
Agonies like knives,entrails
gnawed by coiling snakes,
each breath a quick tongue
of fire raging against his ribs -
the poison from Jezar's arrow
coursing through his veins,
burning all his limbs.

Heavy on his spear, DEATH
will have entered his limbs,
though his dauntless soul
it will have then revered.

In the morning, Antar's armour
still on guard, as his
black stallion Abjer moves
to chase a mare the brigands,
suspicious of Antar's stillness,
will release in front of him,
the suit will topple backwards
to the sand. And after the first
silence of awe following
the death-clang of the armour
against the rocky valley-face
the brigands will circle it,
marvel at the length and size
of man inside, as if he would
leap up and slaughter them
still, from death. Then
they will pick at it
as vultures at a corpse.

While they decorate themselves
with trophies of his steel
and try to catch his horse,
one, softened by the death
of this great warrior,
will cover him with sand and,
weeping, say words for him:
"Defender of his people
in life and death, proclaim
this soul to live forever.
And let the dew freshen
and moisten this his last
warring-place."

         **   **

And Abla will recede
safely into sun and shadows
over the night Antar's vigil
guarded for her, Antar's spirit
firey in her breast.

Just as on her wedding day
she came - pale body
in her robes and gowns -
as if from out of the sky
or the glazed mirror
of the far off desert sand -
the crown of Chosroe on her head,
jewels round her forehead,
through a line of swords
and spears - into a tent
of carpeted sand, of
scented candles - aloes,
ambergris and musk.
Where goat bleats rose

from outside. Where the men
stood breathless, held in awe,
where the women shouted,
stamped their feet, whistled, screamed.

In her hand she brought
an unsheathed sword
that took all breath away
and blinded every eye.

And, after shadows were
once more stilled,
one sideways voice said -
"What a pity that one so beautiful
and white should marry one so black!"

While from the throats
of all the others rose screams
of brute ferocity and awe.

PEACE - PIPE

He sat all night
by the Magpie Tree
smoking a pipe that sent up
spirals of blue smoke
like walls of a house
he would build in the leaves,
seeing them, not quite clearly,
the black and white birds
in the branches and leaves,
counting them, as they called,
or suddenly flew,
like windows he would have
in his house of blue.
Or eyes - one two three
that moved through space
across the river
from willow to elder,
dipping into the meadow,
pools of wild flowers,
the branches and bees,
yellow-flags in the reeds.
One two three irresistibly
from willow to elder
across the wide river,
he saw what he saw.
One two three, then back.
And as he saw what he saw,
three became four.

THIEVES

He stole beneath
the Magpie Tree
where the river
passed still with reeds
and on the wide green bank
meadow cranesbills
flowered, blue mouths
pearled with bees.

He stood on the bank
of rushes and reeds,
smooth as sword blades
by his hands and knees,
watched the birds,
three once more,
fly over the river,
willow to willow,
alder to elder,
their harsh, unmusical call
the same as before
risen from long grass
edging the reservoir.

Then, he saw four. Then,
a thin, black dart,
no movement of the wing,
a fifth bird came,
fleshed with white,
its long tail drawn
clean as a knife through
wafery clouds and light.

Over reeds and cranesbills
blue with bees
across the wide river
he stood looking over
to the edge of the reservoir
swollen with trees
as the bird ended at will,
like the flash in his sight,
in a silvered willow,
its moment of flight.